W9-BHP-585

First Facts®

The Middle Ages

Medieval Knights

by Jim Whiting

Consultant:
James Masschaele
Associate Professor of Medieval History
Rutgers University
New Brunswick, New Jersey

Capstone
press®

Mankato, Minnesota

First Facts is published by Capstone Press,
151 Good Counsel Drive, P.O. Box 669, Mankato, Minnesota 56002.
www.capstonepress.com

Library of Congress Cataloging-in-Publication Data
Whiting, Jim, 1943–
    Medieval knights / by Jim Whiting.
    p. cm. — (First facts. The Middle Ages)
    Includes bibliographical references and index.
    Summary: "Describes medieval knights, including who they were and how they
fought" — Provided by publisher.
    ISBN-13: 978-1-4296-2269-1 (hardcover)
    ISBN-10: 1-4296-2269-5 (hardcover)
    1. Knights and knighthood — Juvenile literature. 2. Civilization, Medieval —
Juvenile literature. I. Title.
CR4513.W48 2009
940.1 — dc22
                                                  2008032331

Editorial Credits

Megan Schoeneberger, editor; Kim Brown, designer; Marcie Spence, photo researcher

Photo Credits

Capstone Press/Karon Dubke, 21; Capstone Press/Kim Brown, 15 (right); Corbis/Blue
Lantern Studio, 9; Corbis/Christie's Images, 12; Getty Images Inc./Peter Macdiarmid,
16–17; iStockphoto/DanielBendjy, 1; Landov LLC/Alexandra Winkler/Reuters, cover;
North Wind Picture Archives, 8, 11, 20; Private Collection/The Bridgeman Art Library
International, 5, 6, 14–15; Shutterstock/Tatiana Morozova, 18

Essential content terms are **bold** and are defined at the bottom of the page where they
first appear.

1 2 3 4 5 6 14 13 12 11 10 09

Table of Contents

Knightly Dreams

In the Middle Ages, boys dreamed of becoming knights. Knights were the warriors of the Middle Ages. They were respected for their strength and courage during battles.

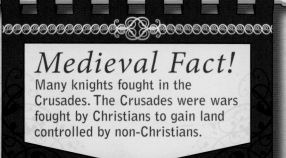

Medieval Fact!

Many knights fought in the Crusades. The Crusades were wars fought by Christians to gain land controlled by non-Christians.

Knights in the Middle Ages
Europe
476 – 1500

English
Knights

French
Knights

Italian
Knights

Spanish
Knights

Who Were Knights?

In the early Middle Ages, any man could become a knight. But he had to use his own weapons and armor. That was expensive. In time, only wealthy men could be knights.

Knights served landowners called **noblemen**. Battles between landowners were common. Knights fought for noblemen. Nobles gave knights land for their service.

nobleman — a wealthy person of high rank

Pages

The path to knighthood began when a boy was about 7 years old. At that age, boys became pages. Pages lived in the home of a knight or nobleman. They ran errands, served food, and hunted. They also learned the fighting skills they would need as knights.

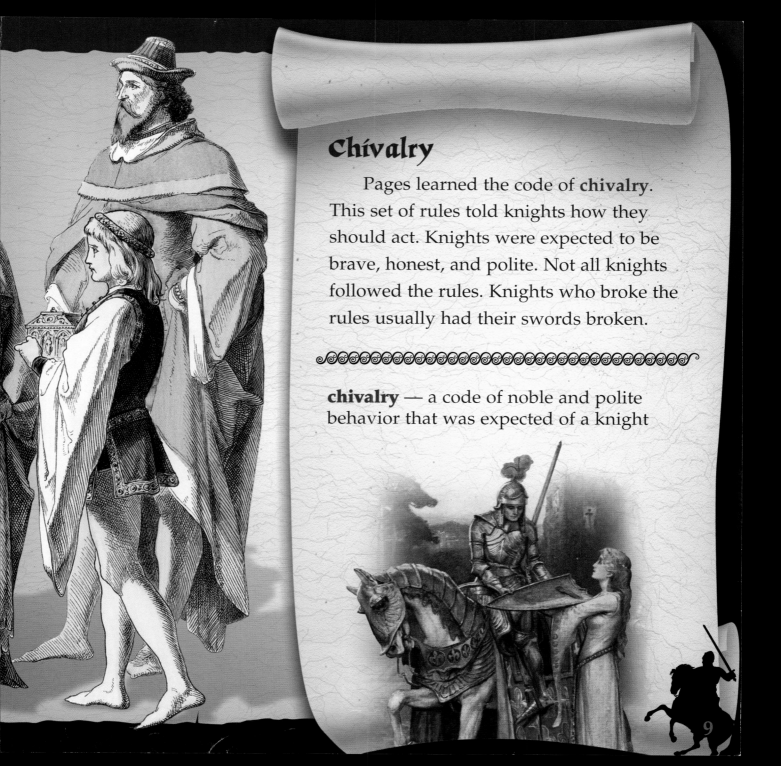

Chivalry

Pages learned the code of **chivalry**. This set of rules told knights how they should act. Knights were expected to be brave, honest, and polite. Not all knights followed the rules. Knights who broke the rules usually had their swords broken.

chivalry — a code of noble and polite behavior that was expected of a knight

Squires

When a boy was about 14, he became a squire. A squire's main job was taking care of his knight's armor. He helped his knight put on armor before a battle. Squires also improved their fighting skills. They sometimes went into battle with their knights.

Medieval Fact!

Even with a squire's help, it took 15 minutes or more to put on a suit of armor.

I Dub Thee Sir Knight

At age 21, a squire became a knight. The ceremony was called **dubbing**. The squire knelt before a crowd of friends and family. He promised to live by the rules of chivalry. A king or queen tapped him with the flat part of a sword. From that point on, the squire was a knight.

dubbing — a ceremony in which a person becomes a knight

Medieval Fact!
Noblemen or other knights could also perform the dubbing ceremony.

The Armor of Knights

For many years, knights wore **chain mail**. This armor weighed about 50 pounds (23 kilograms). But it did not protect against heavy blows. Later on, knights switched to full suits of armor. Steel plates covered each part of a knight's body. A helmet protected his head.

chain mail — thousands of tiny metal rings connected to each other

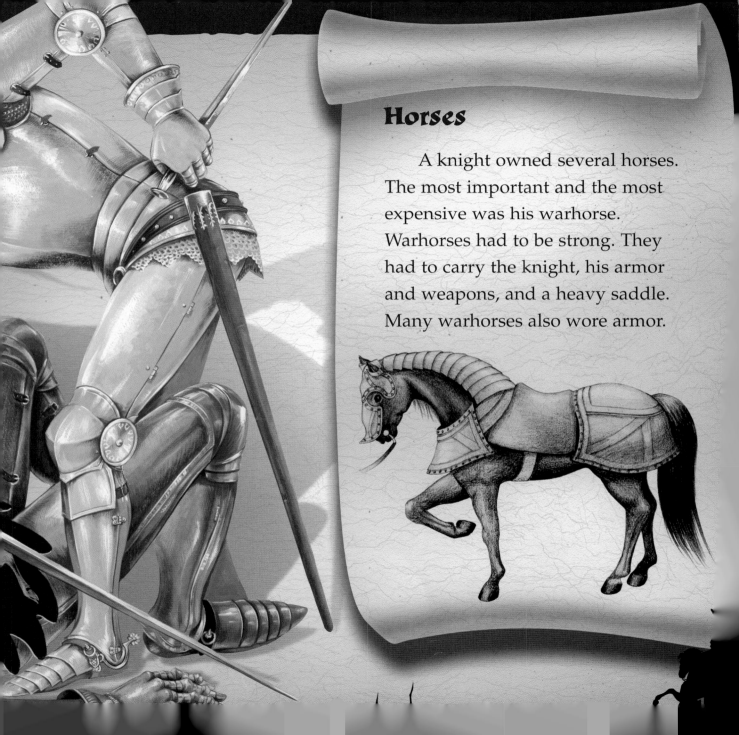

Horses

A knight owned several horses. The most important and the most expensive was his warhorse. Warhorses had to be strong. They had to carry the knight, his armor and weapons, and a heavy saddle. Many warhorses also wore armor.

Tournaments

Knights liked to show off their skills in jousting tournaments. In a joust, two knights rode toward each other as fast as they could. They gripped shields in one hand and long wooden lances in the other. Each knight tried to make the other one tumble off his horse. The loser usually gave his armor to the winner.

Medieval Fact!

In battle, lances had sharp steel tips. For tournaments, the tips were made blunt. That made them much less dangerous.

The End of Knights

Battles changed with guns and cannons. Armor didn't protect knights against bullets and cannonballs. Knights' value as fighters ended.

There are still knights in England today, but they aren't expected to fight. The queen honors important people by making them knights. Actors, singers, and scientists have been dubbed modern knights.

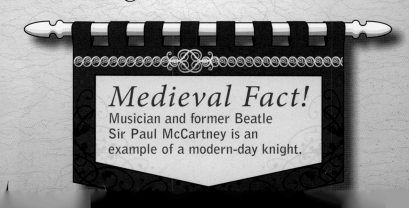

Medieval Fact!

Musician and former Beatle Sir Paul McCartney is an example of a modern-day knight.

Amazing but True!

Knights were hot and uncomfortable in their armor. The steel rubbed knights' skin until it was raw. But sore skin wasn't a knight's biggest problem. Heavy armor made it hard to use a bathroom. Sometimes knights couldn't wait until their armor was off. Their squires cleaned up after them.

Try It Out: Make a Shield

When they put on their armor and helmets, knights all looked the same. They used coats of arms so people could tell them apart. A coat of arms is a design with symbols of things important to each knight. Each coat of arms was different. You can make your own shield with a coat of arms.

What You Need

- pencil
- a large piece of cardboard
- scissors
- ruler
- poster paint
- colored pencils or crayons
- a strip of heavy cardboard
- duct tape

What You Do

1. With an adult helping you, draw the shape of your shield on the large piece of heavy cardboard.
2. Cut out the shield with the scissors.
3. Using the ruler, divide the shield into four sections.
4. Paint each section a different color. You can also use crayons or colored pencils.
5. Draw something important to you in each section with the colored pencils or crayons. If you like soccer, you could draw a soccer ball. Your favorite pet could go in another section. You could also include your initials.
6. When you are finished, attach the cardboard strip with duct tape to make a handle.

Glossary

chain mail (CHAYN MAYL) — armor made up of thousands of tiny iron rings linked together

chivalry (SHIV-uhl-ree) — a code of noble and polite behavior that was expected of a medieval knight

dubbing (DUHB-ing) — a ceremony in which a person becomes a knight

joust (JOUST) — a battle between two knights

lance (LANSS) — a long spear

nobleman (NOH-buhl-muhn) — a wealthy person of high rank

Read More

Adkins, Jan. *What if You Met a Knight?* New Milford, Conn.: Roaring Brook Press, 2006.

Simon, Seymour. *Knights and Castles.* SeeMore Readers. San Francisco: Chronicle Books, 2006.

Steer, Dugald. *Knight: A Noble Guide for Young Squires.* Cambridge, Mass.: Candlewick Press, 2006.

Weintraub, Aileen. *Knights: Warriors of the Middle Ages.* Way of the Warrior. New York: Children's Press, 2005.

Internet Sites

FactHound offers a safe, fun way to find educator-approved Internet sites related to this book.

Here's what you do:
1. Visit *www.facthound.com*
2. Choose your grade level.
3. Begin your search.

This book's ID number is 9781429622691.

FactHound will fetch the best sites for you!

Index